Crisis Communication

Or
Don't Let Your Hair Catch on Fire!

By
Doc Kokol

Crisis Communication
Don't Let your Hair Catch on Fire!

Copyright © 2017 by Kokol and Associates, LLC

All rights reserved. This book or any portion thereof may not be reproduced or used in any manner whatsoever without the express written permission of the publisher except for the use of brief quotations in a book review.

Printed in the United States of America
ISBN-13:978-1985049222
ISBN-10:1985049228

Kokol and Associates, LLC
2107 Gibbs Drive
Tallahassee, FL 32303
www.kokolandassociates.com

Table of Contents

What the heck does he know? 1
Do this first 3
Build your team 4
Incident Command Structure 6
It's 10 o'clock... do you know where
    your staff is? 9
But they will panic! 12
Message Maps 14
Message Map Template 15
You know 90% of the questions you are going
    to be asked 16
Just what is risk? 17
How to build a plan that FAILS! 22
Push, not pull 28
Anatomy of a Risk and Crisis Event 29
Some final advice 37

What the heck does he know?

This book draws on my 40 plus years of experience putting out fires for government and private sector companies. Everything I am going to suggest or propose is based on that experience; the good and more importantly the bad. The information provided is based on several "career-altering moments" I have survived. Moments like anthrax attacks, cancer clusters, pandemic flu scares, massive oil spills, Chinese drywall, bear attacks, python invasions… to name a few of the more exciting moments.

The most important advice I can give you is simple and straight forward, but difficult to carry out when you, and your boss is running about like your hair is on fire.

Tell the truth, tell it all at once and tell people how to protect themselves, their family and their pets.

Also, tell them how you are going to fix this problem. Why would I include pets? Having been part of teams working on hurricanes and wildfires, I have spoken to people who refused to evacuate, would not leave their homes in the face of imminent danger because they could not take their pets with them to a shelter. Just a note, most jurisdictions now have shelters that are pet friendly.

There are lots of risk and crisis books written by experts in the field. Many will provide you with the academic research of how people react to risk and crisis stimuli, or the psychology of fear. If that's what you are looking for, this is not the book for you. If you want a survival guide, a short plain-language map of how to get through this crisis with as little pain for you and your boss as possible, while providing important and sometimes vital information to your clients and the public then you have come to the right place.

Do this first

You need to have a conversation with your leadership that may be difficult for them. Be gentle, but get the information you need... now. The premise of this conversation is "I can't help you if I don't know what's over the horizon". There is an old saying "PR Division, last to know... first to go. You can substitute Communications division and it holds just as true. If someone is about to be indicted, a product is going to be recalled, employees are going to be fired or arrested you need to know now. It's really upsetting to learn about these things in the newspaper, or on Facebook. Some of you are thinking... really, I bought a book to tell me to meet with my boss... but many of you still need to schedule this meeting.

How did the meeting go? Most people find one or two nuggets that will help in their planning and may even find the "bad thing". You know when your boss started with "I didn't want you to tell anyone about this...but." So, you have your list of items that may become issues. Find the item that you REALLY don't want to happen, the one that gives you bad feelings in your stomach... and work on that one first. Trust me.

Build your team

You can't do this alone. Really, you can't. You need a team to make a Risk and Crisis Communication plan work. Find your subject matter experts first. Here is where the term "plain-language" comes in. There are experts who know their field and experts who know their field and can explain it in simple to understand language.

Early in my career, I worked for a major state university. I had the opportunity to meet a Nobel prize winner in physics who gave me this advice. "True experts in their field can explain very complex ideas in simple language… but there are pretenders who hide behind technical jargon to mask their lack of knowledge." A critical part of your work will be to bring subject matter experts together to explain to you, so you can tell the public, what is going on. It doesn't matter if it's financial information, or why this year's flu vaccine isn't effective; you need to help them focus on plain language so you can build an effective message. I like to use the probing phrase, "So why should I care?"

You may get lucky and find a subject matter expert who seems like he or she would do well in front of a camera. Maybe they already meet with the media for interviews and press conferences. Proceed with caution. They will also be the person answering questions from the media. No matter how smooth or agile they seem, set aside time to brief them, and hold a mock interview, as real as you can, to see how they do.

As best as you can, make sure the soon to be on-camera subject matter expert doesn't have a hidden agenda. The rule should be no surprises. I once prepped a respected scientist for an interview with Associated Press about flu and the need for vaccinations. He had the talking points down cold. Everything was going great until he decided to volunteer that "statistically" 360,000 or more Floridians might die in a pandemic flu event. As the Communications maven, your standing off to the side, smiling and thinking about pulling the building fire alarm, just to stop what started as a great interview. AP had a great quote, the scientist told me later that he did that to "raise awareness" of pandemic flu. The Governor had to travel the state to calm Floridians. This one was close to a career-altering moment.

Once you have identified your subject matter experts, work on your communications team. You will need staff to answer the phones, manage your website, and critical to your success and your company's survival, staff to monitor, post and respond to social media.

In the "good old days" when an event occurred, our team would meet, decide on the message, invite the media to a press conference, put out the information and answer questions. Oh, how I loved the good old days! Now you will likely learn about the event or crisis on social media, with videos and pictures…lots of pictures.

What a great transition to why you need to prepare ahead of time.

Incident Command System

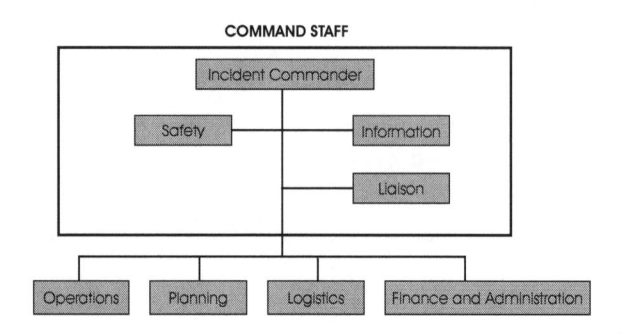

```
                    COMMAND STAFF
         ┌─────────────────────────────────┐
         │       Incident Commander        │
         │   Safety ──┬── Information      │
         │            ├── Liaison          │
         └──┬──────┬──┴──┬──────────┬──────┘
            │      │     │          │
       Operations Planning Logistics Finance and Administration
```

No matter the size of your company or agency, no matter how well you work together or how much like a family you are, during a crisis people start stepping on each other's toes.

Fortunately, over the years, public and private sector organizations have created a template that works when stuff is hitting the fan. It's called the Incident Command System (ICS).

An incident command system, designed, approved and practiced ahead of the crisis keeps you from bumping into each other and losing your public's confidence. Remember, you can modify the titles in section blocks to fit your business.

The Incident Command System is a tool used for the command, control, and coordination of your event. It's all about resource (people, equipment, and dollars) management, which is very important in a crisis, especially one that takes time to resolve.

ICS is scalable, it can be made larger or smaller as your event needs, and it can be done "virtually" by computer or phone if needed. Don't let the labels in the boxes put you off. There is nothing magical about them. Change the titles as needed, but keep the concept intact. You might not need a safety officer unless your event involves staff in the field doing things that might be dangerous. Before you delete the Safety Officer because "We don't do dangerous stuff", consider the emotional toll your event is going to have on staff, and the help a Safety Officer can provide making sure staff goes home and rests, shifts are equitable and people take time to eat. If you are the PIO for a nuclear plant…. well, you will have a busy safety officer.

The Liaison officer is there to coordinate the input from other agencies, in some cases that might be other factory locations or it could be other government agencies. Make it fit your needs.

Please note that the Public Information Officer (PIO), in the Information block on the chart, reports directly to the Incident Commander. You do not want someone to interpret the needs of the Incident Commander before it gets to the PIO or the alternative, someone filtering the needs of the Incident Commander to the PIO.

It's common sense not to introduce something new like an incident command system during an incident to staff who have never seen it before. There is a wealth of information about ICS on the web, take time to get familiar with it. Here is just one site

https://emilms.fema.gov/is100b/ics01summary.htm

It's 10 o'clock... do you know where your staff is?

Some of you may be old enough to remember the PSA that ran on local television stations (remove staff and insert children in the headline above).

Really, your phone rings in the middle of the night and you learn of the incident. It's always in the middle of the night... if it's day... well, it seems to turn to night. You need to call your staff, so you go to your purse or wallet and get out your handy staff home and cell phone list. What... you don't have one... or it's so old the home numbers listed are still landlines... get that done now. Depending on the size of your staff you may want to create a call-down list. You call Bill who calls Susan, Lena and James. They each call 3 people. You see how it goes.

OK, what do you want your staff to do at 10 o'clock at night? Can they work from home, do you have the conference call-in numbers and passwords, who do you need in the office now, and who can wait to come in later? If you can, stagger your staff, this may be a multi-day or longer event and you don't want to burn people out.

Make sure your boss knows what is going on... and that you are on it. Here is where things get interesting. You (or your boss) needs to pull decision makers into the same room as soon as possible. That likely means tonight, not tomorrow when it's convenient, like after the standing weekly leadership meeting.

Listen carefully, there are NO secrets. Say that again out loud. There are NO secrets. Your event is on social media already, with video and pictures... lots of pictures. If you haven't gotten media calls, it's just that they can't find you...yet. Someone from your firm or agency needs to stand up and let the public know the basics.

It's very early, you just learned about the incident, and you are still gathering the facts.

This are a fluid event and information and data is likely to change.

Here is what we know right now.

I will be back at (fill in the time) with an update.

Remember the basics, tell the truth, tell it all at once and tell people how to protect themselves, their family and their pets. Depending on your event, adapt this message as necessary.

If you don't have a telephone conferencing system, one that does not take operator assistance, get one now. Some of them are "free" some offer a toll-free call-in number. When bad stuff is happening, it may be your most valuable tool.

Do the people you need to talk to during a crisis carry a cell phone? I know, everyone has a cell phone, but just test the assumption. Many people have a cell phone provided by work, you know, so you can get up with them when you need to. Email or text sometime at 9 or 10 at night and see who responds, and when. If necessary show them how to put a unique ring on their phone for critical calls or emails. It's not hard, and if you make it a really ugly ring, you might get their attention.

But they will panic!

Don't be surprised if after gathering the facts someone in the room doesn't opine "if we send this out the public will PANIC!" Sound familiar? There have been several studies that indicate people running in the street in full-blown panic is very rare. What those in the know see as panic are people who don't have the information you do and are responding with this lack of knowledge in a survival mode.

Remember this. People want to know what YOU know that keeps YOU from panicking. If there is information that you have that lowers your concern about the impact or long-term effect... let the public know.

It might go something like this. A recent sampling of our water supply indicates the presence of kryptonite. Laboratory experiments have shown kryptonite can cause cancer in rats. The rest of the story is that kryptonite is always found in water supplies, and the level found is so low it is not a health threat. The lab tests fed rats half their body weight of kryptonite. To the scientists out there, I made this up. I don't know if there really is kryptonite or not. Or how about this.

Public Health authorities report that workers at the Really Big Cattle Farm, located in the eastern part of this county, have tested positive for anthrax exposure. You might also want to tell the public that; "You cannot catch anthrax from another person the way you might catch a cold or the flu. In rare cases, person-to-person transmission has been reported with cutaneous anthrax, where discharges from skin lesions might be infectious" *Centers for Disease Control and Prevention*

If you live in the eastern part of the county and you are only told the first part of that statement, your reaction might be different, maybe even look like panic, then if you have all the information.
Remember that not saying anything about the Kryptonite or anthrax will not work. There are no secrets!

Message Maps

Message maps will keep your hair from catching on fire. Great visual isn't it. During my career of managing risk and crisis communications events, nothing has proven more useful than message maps.

Message maps and the template I use in this book was created by Dr. Vincent T. Covello, Ph.D. of the Center for Risk Communication, and used with his permission, *www.centerforriskcommunication.org*

Thank you, Dr. Covello, for the great work you have done in this field and mentoring a generation of Risk and Crisis Communicators.

Message maps are based on research that found most television sound bites are 9 seconds long, and most people will speak 27 words in 9 seconds.

Studies have also found that under stress your audience will retain 3 key points. The basis for message maps is 3/27/9. Three key points, 27 words and nine seconds. It also seems that most opening paragraphs in a newspaper article are about 27 words long.

Ok, I can see some of you starting to send me emails that go something like this. "Ha… I found an opening paragraph in the Daily Bugle that is 43 words long…." People… it's a guide.

The world will continue to turn if you use 31 words or it takes you 32 seconds to give your three points. But, if we know this is the average, and we want to get OUR quote in the paper or on air, why not give the reporter what they need?

Message Map Template

What is Prescribed Fire?

Key Message 1	Key Message 2	Key Message 3
Prescribed fire is a safe way to apply a natural process	**A way to ensure ecosystem health**	**A method to reduce wildfire risk**
Supporting Fact 1-1	Supporting Fact 2-1	Supporting Fact 3-1
Historically fire is a natural regular event.	**Restores and improves wildlife habitat**	**Reduces dangerous buildup of brush and forest debris**
Supporting Fact 1-2	Supporting Fact 2-1	Supporting Fact 3-2
Many Plants and animals depend on fire to thrive	**Replenishes soil nutrients**	**Makes wildfire less intense and destructive**
Supporting Fact 1-3	Supporting Fact 2-2	Supporting Fact 3-3
Trained professionals use science to mimic a natural process	**Helps maintain a diverse and healthy forest**	**Produces less smoke than a wildfire.**

During your interview or press conference, the key message becomes your safe harbor. It reads this way. "Prescribed fire, is a safe way to apply a natural process, that ensures ecosystem health and reduces wildfire risk." Done. That's your statement. If you have more time, use the supporting facts to prove this statement. The supporting statements are read down the column. "Historically fire is a natural, regular event, many plants and animals depend on fire to thrive, and trained professionals use science to mimic a natural process."

You know 90% of the questions you are going to be asked.

If you sit down and think about it, you and your subject matter experts know 90% of the questions you are going to be asked during an interview or at a press conference. That knowledge becomes the basis for your message maps. What are we likely to be asked, and what is our answer going to be? What, you don't have time to build message maps during an event? Your right. Build them when things are calm. The basic questions won't change. Remember this; work on the questions you don't want to answer first! I know, I told you that before.... maybe it's really important.

During the calm, make time to build message maps for the questions that you know will be asked. If you're a bank, what you are going to say if you are robbed, or a staff member steals money. If you're a Health Department, you have a list of horribles... kids in school testing positive for TB, flu outbreak and no flu vaccine. If you're a nuclear power plant, well .... I think you can figure it out.

Don't hesitate to build these message maps now. You can modify them as needed. Get your review team to approve them. Put them in a binder and keep one copy at work and one at home. Consider building web pages that are kept offline until they are needed. The one precious commodity during a crisis is time. You won't have time to do the foundational items well and keep up with the demands of the event at the same time. Do it now.

Just what is risk?

So, what exactly is risk? It is a threat to what we value. It is personalized and unique to the individual. It is important to note that the risk that will harm or hurt us and the risk that scares us are often completely different. There is no logic behind the ranking of what can hurt or kill us and what we fear. Here is just one example. People are afraid of being struck by lightning, but not so much about obesity. Guess which one kills more people

Dr. Peter Sandman, www.psandman.com one of the experts whose work I recommend, defines risk as hazard plus outrage.

Hazard + Outrage = Risk

High Risk, Low Outrage

Some instances are high hazard and low outrage. Like wearing your seat belt when you drive or a personal flotation device when boating. The likelihood of being hurt is very high if you don't comply, but the outrage is low. In this scenario, you have an apathetic audience, and it's hard to capture and hold their attention. They don't care.

Low Risk, High Outrage

There are also situations of low risk, but very high outrage. The most challenging event I ever worked was a cancer cluster that involved children. The risk to the community was very low, but the outrage was very high. Statistically, there was slight increase in pediatric cancers in a neighborhood. Parents were afraid to let their children take a bath, or go outside to play. Parents with children diagnosed with cancer were convinced it had to be something in the water, air or soil. The media made this story their lead for months, to the point that banks refused to offer mortgages or loans in this community thinking it was going to be a Love Canal event. The community became divided, those who believed there was something wrong with their environment and those who felt everything was ok. The "unbelievers" thought the furor was centered in one or two families, and because of them, everyone's property values were going in the tank.

If you are working an event like this you can expect those affected to turn their fear and anger towards you and your agency. There is usually a core group of "true believers" and a larger group that is less outraged who will watch to see how the controversy evolves. Public meetings with the audience doing most of the talking seem to be the most effective method of managing a low-risk high outrage event. Be prepared to be the point of their anger and fear.

Moderate Risk, Moderate Outrage

In a moderate risk, moderate outrage situation, the public is likely uninterested or unconcerned, but specialty groups and stakeholders become the attentive audience. Stakeholder groups need to be brought inside during your planning meetings so they can see your decision-making process. This may be the only scenario where you will want to be prepared to answer very technical questions, with details. Generally, these are not media events, but a stakeholder group that does not feel like they have your attention or are part of the "team" can change that.

An example of moderate risk, moderate outrage is red tide. Oh, you don't know about red tide? See what I mean. Red tide is very important to Florida coastal communities. It is an algal bloom that can cause respiratory issues for some. If you are the President of a Chamber of Commerce, or beach front hotel owner, or the local allergy doctor, red tide is important to you because most people don't want to go to a beach that has a Red Tide, and it bothers some people's health. Some believe Red Tide comes from excessive fertilizer use and its runoff into bodies of water, but others note that Red Tide was documented by early explorers like Cabeza de Vaca, and I don't think there was much commercial fertilization going on in the mid-1500's. Stay connected with your stakeholders and have your subject matter experts close to answer the "in the weeds" questions.

High Risk, High Outrage

This is the real deal. This is when people are in danger, and they are upset. Rule number one… don't over-reassure. At this point, you don't know if everything is going to be OK so don't tell the public it is. Never, ever tell people who are scared… they have nothing to be scared about. Once again, all together…Let people know what they can do to protect themselves, their family and their pets.

Provide options for people in this situation. You MUST do X. You SHOULD do Y, and you CAN do Z. Usually, the public does not direct its outrage at you early in a high-risk high outrage event, but once the event is over, you will hear things like: Why didn't you prepare or predict better. Couldn't it have been fixed quicker and cost less? Who was responsible for this mess… I want a name!

An example of a High-Risk High Outrage event is the story of an exotic animal park owner in Ohio who let all his animals loose and then committed suicide. Animals that ran free included Bengal tigers, leopards, grizzly bears, and lions. While this was in a rural area, schools had to be closed, residents warned to stay inside and protect their families and pets.

People were told they MUST stay inside, they were told they SHOULD bring their pets inside, and they CAN stay informed by tuning to "WXXX" on their radio.

News reports after the event indicated that Ohio had some of the weakest restrictions on exotic pet rules and was among the highest in injuries and deaths from exotic animals. The Humane Society of the United States criticized the Governor for letting a ban on the sale and importation of buying or selling exotic pets expire. Questions along the line of "how many people will have to be injured or die before something is done are common after this kind of event.

How to build a plan that FAILS!

Here are some clear benchmarks that will cause your Risk and Crisis Communication plan to fail.

Be smart, and don't do them.

Mixed Messages

One of the easiest ways for your plan to blow up is for your agency, firm or workplace to put out mixed messages. Often, it's the unofficial messages that get you in trouble. Interviews you don't know about, you know when staff says, "well the reporter called me... what was I supposed to do... hang up"? Or the "Oh I didn't know you put out talking points", kind of messages. Get everyone on the same page, as quickly as possible. If you are part of a State or Federal agency, you will have a Joint Information Center (JIC) as part of your incident command center.

A Joint Information Center (JIC) is a part of the Incident Command System (ICS) we discussed earlier. It is a gathering of the communication teams from all the agencies involved in the event, either in person or by phone or computer. Its purpose is to make sure that one message being put out by one group does not conflict with another group's message. No one loses their identity, it just makes everyone play nice together.

A good example of mixed messages, the kind you want to avoid, is an incident after a hurricane. There were at least three government agencies putting out fact sheets about how to treat water so it is safe to drink. Each one listed the use of chlorine bleach in the process, and each one had a different formula of bleach to water. This does not inspire confidence in the public.

The public doesn't want to "pick one message" from many messages. They need one clear voice. That's you. You need to expect unofficial experts to pop up to offer advice. I recommend reaching out to these unofficial experts and bring them into the fold. Give them the same talking points you are giving your team. Let them continue to have their voice, but try to have that voice amplify your message, not compete with it.

Information released late

If a reporter calls and says his or her deadline is 5 o'clock, you do understand that you are not the only source he or she is reaching out to… don't you? If you don't respond, it just means you don't get to tell your side of the story… and you might be noted as "did not reply" or the dreaded… "refused to comment". If you can't meet the deadline, let the reporter know why not, and when you think you can. If you will NEVER give him the answer, try the "no but" response. "I am sorry, but this is an active investigation, or state statute won't allow me to give out that information, or we don't have that information now… BUT WHAT I CAN TELL YOU IS…

In a crisis situation, there is a tendency to delay the release of information until you have all the details. Every one of them. Often times this suggestion comes from the attorneys involved. Here is what I suggest. Tell the public things are changing quickly... but this is what you know now. Remember the idea of telling the public what you know that keeps you from being afraid. Let your audience know that as new, verified information comes in you will update them, and let them know how you will update them... web page, press conference, email, whatever your method is.

I think the key point is that there is a conversation going on about your company or agency. If you want to be a part of that conversation you need to get out in front. If you don't, people will talk about you anyway. Sort of like talking behind your back. The communication principles from the CDC are:

1. Be First: Crises are time-sensitive. Communicating information quickly is almost always important. For members of the public, the first source of information often becomes the preferred source.
2. Be Right: Accuracy establishes credibility. Information can include what is known, what is not known, and what is being done to fill in the gaps.
3. Be Credible: Honesty and truthfulness should not be compromised during crises.
4. Express Empathy: Crises create harm, and the suffering should be acknowledged in words. Addressing what people are feeling, and the challenges they face builds trust and rapport.

5. Promote Action: Giving people meaningful things to do calms anxiety, helps restore order, and promotes a restored sense of control.
6. Show Respect: Respectful communication is particularly important when people feel vulnerable. Respectful communication promotes cooperation and rapport.

Paternalistic attitudes

There... there, you don't have anything to worry about, we have got this covered. Don't ever tell someone who is scared that there is nothing to be scared about. Maybe if they had the information you have they won't be scared, so tell them. During a crisis, people need to feel like they have some control over their fate. Give them something to do, you must, you can, you should, as well as lead with the information you have that keeps you from being scared. You can replace scared with concerned, angry etc. to fit the situation. Please do not tell people "know how you feel". No, you don't.

Not countering rumors and myths in real time

Rumors and myths are not new to risk and crisis communications, but their importance has been amplified by social media and electronic publishing. Not only does everyone think they are an expert, in all fields, but now they have a worldwide instant platform to let others know just how expert they are. Or perhaps more damaging, they can remain anonymous while spreading rumors that can cause the public to make dangerous decisions.

Rumors and myths must be attended to quickly as the media will report rumors or hoaxes as facts unless you can show them why it is false. How do you counter the rumors and myths? First, you need an open, quick reliable channel to the media. So, use the same instant communication formats that the rumor mongers do. Facebook, twitter, and email.

You can't start a social media network during a crisis, you have to develop it during the calm. It needs to be the normal place the media and the public look for information from your organization. Once that is in place all your press releases or messaging to the public should include social media as a distribution channel. In addition, build a rumor and myth web page now, but hold off publishing it until you need it.

One way to counter myths and rumors is to have a central place to send the public and the media that addresses these rumors and lays out the facts. During the event, when someone posts a comment that is not true, counter it on your Facebook or twitter page and send interested parties to your rumor and myth web site, where they can see this rumor and your response as well as the other rumors you have found. This site also gives the public and the media the opportunity to see other myths and rumors, unrelated to theirs. It's time-consuming, but it is essential.

Most social media outlets are "self-regulating" in that other community members will counter rumors and myths, but some rumors have just enough "possibility" in it that you need to stop them as quickly as possible, or they will grow legs.

Public power struggles and conflict

Nothing degrades public confidence faster than elected or appointed officials fussing at each other in public. Not long ago, a hurricane was headed to a city that had not been visited by a hurricane in many years.

The mayor of the city was considering running for Governor of the State. The sitting Governor of the state, representing a different party, was not a great fan of the Mayor. The storm came and caused significant damage to the power grid of this city and the Governor reached out to the Mayor and asked if he could help with resources and expertise. The Mayor basically told the Governor to "butt out. we got this". In much nicer terms, I'm sure.

People were suffering, power was off and the Governor was wondering why the Mayor had turned down his offer for more utility workers from other cities and regions to come help. All of this played out in the media. Not the way to build confidence in the ability of government or any organization to manage a crisis.

A press conference can be another source of public struggle and conflict if it has not been planned out and all parties agree to the ground rules. Jockeying for mike or worse, that awkward moment when a hard question is asked and everyone plays like the mike disappeared, or they need to check their smart phone... are symptoms of power struggles and conflict.

Push, not pull

"We will put the information up on our webpage, and the public can keep up to date". This is a lot like "if you build it they will come". Nope, it doesn't work. You need to push information out to your public. How do you do that?

Now is the time to have a chat with your IT director, or whoever manages your web page and social media feeds. If you are not currently using the internet and social media-driven programs, please reach out to a local consultant. It will be one of the foundational parts of your risk and crisis communication plan. There are several methods to push information out to your public, but it's hard to start the process during the event.

The simplest method of pushing out information are email addresses and text messages. You can build your own stakeholder and audience list by putting sign-up information on everything you send to the public. Invoices, newsletters, the back of business cards, yes you can have them printed on both sides, your Facebook page and most important your web page. The most successful method I have found in gathering email addresses is a pop-up box that shows up the first time someone visits your website. By using the magic of cookies, you can limit the pop-up box to first-time visitors. Give them the chance to put in their email address or text cell number, and then make sure you confirm through a follow-up email that they really want to sign up.

I recommend talking to your IT help to identify a commercial email vendor who can automate most of these capture items as well as manage the transmission side.

Anatomy of a Risk and Crisis Event

The Acreage Pediatric Cancer Cluster, Palm Beach County Florida

This 2009-10 event was one of the most complex and difficult communication projects I have ever worked on. While this event is clearly a health risk event, the basics of the response, as well as the outreach, can serve as an example of how a complex event can be managed, and in some cases mismanaged. This response combined messages, politics, national media, dueling experts, con artists, children and the ever-present human response to a personal crisis into one giant hot mess. In the beginning of this book, I told you that one of the best learning avenues is to see what didn't work. This did not start well.

This is not a day to day overview of the event, but a review of the highlights of the risk and crisis response; what worked, what didn't work and why. A simple internet search for Acreage Cancer Cluster will provide you with the day to day health and political events that took place. I was the Communications Director for the Florida Department of Health (DOH) during this event; responsible for our risk messaging, media management and I also served as the DOH representative at the Acreage Community meetings that took place from 2009 to 2010 so I will limit my outline to the risk and crisis event and leave the political aspects to others more qualified.

The event can be summed up in a statement by an upset Mother "God did not intend my child to have cancer, it must be something in air or soil, it can't just be chance."

The beginning

It started with an email from a resident in the Acreage whose child had brain cancer. Through a series of happen stance meetings, she learned that other children in her neighborhood had cancer. She mentioned this to her child's physician and he recommended she contact the Florida Department of Health. She did, and that email started a process that changed the face of a community, pitted neighbor against neighbor and put the Acreage front and center of a media, legal, political and emotional war.

There was a plan in place at DOH to manage inquiry like this. The email went to one of our epidemiologists or disease detectives. They provided the mother with forms to capture more information about her child's cancer and to provide to other neighbors who also had pediatric cancer in their family. DOH received inquiry like this from time to time and in most cases, there was no follow up to the request for more data. It didn't take long for the media to get wind of these forms and write a story about DOH gathering information about kids with cancer in the Acreage.

While talking to a reporter who was calling about the forms we provided the Mother, the epidemiologists said the magic words, "Cancer Cluster". We didn't know at the time if there was a cancer cluster; defined by the CDC as a "greater than expected number of cancer cases that occurs within a group of people in a geographic area over a period of time", but you couldn't take those words back. Now it starts.

The Community, the media, and the politicians wanted answers…today, and I was slow in recognizing the impact the words "Cancer Cluster" would have.

Parents were calling and asking some very simple direct questions… can my baby bathe in our water… can I let them play in our yard… how could you let this happen? I didn't have the answers, there was confusion about who said what to the media. I didn't know that if history is an indicator, the cause of most cancer clusters is never found, unless you agree that chance can be a choice.

Things started to move quickly at DOH, but not quick enough. The media reached out to our County Health Director, DOH has offices in each of Florida's 67 counties. The Director was a physician, and very good at her job. When asked by the media when we were planning to start testing water soil and environment, she told them that we were not. She explained that the source of most if not all cancer clusters are never located, and it was a waste of resources to just "test for everything" without a clue as to what we were looking for. She mentioned that cell phones, and processed meat are thought to cause cancer. It didn't go well with the Acreage community or their elected officials.

How not to hold a public meeting

It was clear that DOH needed to reach out to the public and provide them with the most reliable information available. Elected officials were fuming that we had not done so already, after a week of media stories. They helped us by setting the time and date and letting the public know there would be a meeting to answer their questions. Basically, make it all better.

Instead of taking Dr. Sandman's advice and holding a meeting with interest stations, we decided on holding a town hall meeting in the local high school auditorium. State legislators wanted to be involved, but the legislature was in session, so they decided they would be brought in by live video link. The visual the audience got was a stage full of experts from DOH, and a huge video screen with the face of the legislator looming behind them. I was not able to attend.

There was public speculation about radiation being the cause of the cancers. DOH had a Radiation Division, with real experts; why not ask them to make a presentation, in fact, let them lead off. It might have been good to get examples of the presentation plan ahead of time. It didn't go well.

The audience wanted to know if their children were being poisoned by radiation, the expert wanted to give them a magical mystery tour of the art and science of radiation. At one point, the looming face of the legislator told him to stop; unfortunately, our radiation expert felt it necessary to continue since he wasn't done yet, he made it clear he didn't like being interrupted. I was watching this on live television, it was a train wreck and got worse.

We didn't know that a famous environment plaintiff attorney held a community meeting the day before ours, and told the audience that DOH was going to stall, going to tell half-truths, and it was their job to confront us and make us do the work. Her message resonated with our audience.

The media had a field day showing footage and stills of concerned community members shaking their fists and yelling, not talking loud but yelling at the people on the stage. It was so bad that I got a text message from the leader on stage asking me if I can arrange a security detail so they could get to their cars when the event was over.

So, what should we have done? Here is some information from Dr. Paul Sandman, an expert in Outrage Management. www.psandman.com

"Most of the people at the meeting are upset – angry or frightened or both.

What they're upset about is a foregone conclusion, or at least they think it is. Decisions have been made that meeting participants oppose. They want to reverse those decisions, but they doubt they can accomplish that goal via persuasion. They hope to accomplish it via political action.

Participants may be upset at each other – that is, divided on key issues. But usually, they are mostly on one side, upset at the decision-makers. People who support the decision-makers are less likely to show up for the meeting, as are people who don't care much either way.

Participants' chief reason for being there is to vent – to voice their objections in the presence of each other, the decision-makers they're upset with, and journalists who can help them spread the word.

While the participants are there voluntarily, the decision-makers have come to the meeting because they cannot avoid it. Their goal is to protect their prior decisions, to avoid giving ground. Their other goal, which conflicts with the first, is to calm people down.

The substantive issues are minor compared to the emotional issues. The outcomes participants fear most are considered unlikely by technical experts.

Participants find it easy to believe those outcomes are likely mostly because the decision-makers have been (and continue to be) arrogant, over-reassuring, dismissive, unresponsive, and not quite honest."

What we should have done

The event was a clear moment of low risk and high outrage. Rather than open the meeting "lecturing" about radiation and how it's everywhere, we should have spent time actively listening to the audience, and letting them vent.

Until the audience is convinced we are really listening to them, and value their input, they will not listen to what we had to say. From the community's perspective, the purpose of this meeting was to vent, to yell at DOH, to let us know how upset they were. When they are done they wanted to hear that we were listening and are aware of the concerns and challenges of the Community. And they wanted to know just what we were going to do about it.

It was not the time to argue about junk points. You may feel compelled to correct items that push your hot button. Don't. Listen to what the group is saying, let them know that you have heard them, and then lay out your plan.

What we did right

Things got better. We started meeting the needs of this Community and concentrating on providing plain language information and advice for people who were scared of the water their children were drinking and the air they were breathing.

DOH participated in the *Acreage Focus Group*, a local group made up of residents and elected officials. I was selected to be the DOH member of this stakeholder group; my role was to find answers to the questions they had and identify and invite subject matter experts to visit with this concerned and motivated audience. The challenge with this organization was the makeup.

While the community was divided, those who thought there was something wrong with the environment, and those who thought the cluster was due to chance, the chance believers did not participate in the Focus Group. There was no balancing view against those who were positive their air, water, and dirt was poisoned.

We also opened a storefront in a local shopping center. The Help Office was staffed with a registered nurse, and an epidemiologist, 7 days a week, late afternoon and evening. I believe this was the action that convinced the Community that DOH was with them for the long haul and had their best interest at heart.

It was expensive, staff was not happy having to work weekends and evening, but the Community loved it, and in turn, put away their pitchforks and flaming torches... sort of. The Help Office provided an opportunity for community members to ask questions in private; without a crowd listening to your families most personal details. It let community members ask any question they had without fear of ridicule from others. It provided a professional, personal touch that this community needed badly.

Some final advice

Build your team now. Don't wait.

Find out what keeps your boss up at night

When you stand up in front of the community or the press keep it simple

Tell the Truth

Tell it all at once

Tell people how to protect themselves, their family and their pets

Tell them what you know that keeps you from being afraid, and

Tell them when you will be back with more information.

Rinse and repeat as often as needed.

I hope this guide will help you prepare and manage the next risk and crisis event headed your way, or help you avoid one. Part 2 of this package has the snappy title "How to Keep a Media Interview from Becoming an Interrogation" and will soon be available at Kindle Books. If you would like to know when this book is available, please visit www.kokolandassociates.com and sign up for future announcements.

Message mapping is much easier with a template. If you want a free template, just send me an email at doc@kokolandassociates.com and I will send the file along to you.

If you have any comments or suggestions, please visit my web page at kokolandassociates.com or send me a note at doc@kokolandassociates.com and please take a minute to leave a review on Kindle good or bad. I think this information is important, if you do too, please let others know. If it was a waste of time, feel free to let them know that as well.

Part 2 of this package has the snappy title Surviving a Media Interview, Interview or Interrogation… Your Choice! Is available at Kindle Books in digital and print format.

Please visit www.kokolandassociates.com and sign up for future announcements.

Made in the USA
Middletown, DE
09 June 2025